Teacher's Guide and Answer Key

VOCABULARY
FROM
CLASSICAL
ROOTS

A

Norma Fifer ▾ Nancy Flowers

Educators Publishing Service, Inc.

Cambridge and Toronto

Cover photograph by Katharine Klubock

ISBN 0-8388-2253-3
May 2000 Printing

Contents

Notes on Using *Vocabulary from Classical Roots**

1. **Latin (L.) and Greek (G.) forms.** Complete sets of these forms help to explain the spelling of their English derivatives. Practice pronouncing these words by following some simple rules.

   To pronounce Latin:
   Every *a* sounds like *ah*, as in *swan*.
   The letter *v* is pronounced like *w*.
   The letter *e* at the end of a word, as in the verb *amare*, should sound like the *e* in *egg*.

   To pronounce Greek:
   As in Latin, *a* sounds like *ah*.
   The diphthong *ei* rhymes with *say*; for example, the verb *agein* rhymes with *rain*.
   Au, as in *autos*, sounds like the *ow* in *owl*, and *os* rhymes with *gross*.

2. **Diacritical marks.** Following every defined word in *Vocabulary from Classical Roots* is the guide to pronunciation, as in (dī ə krĭt´ ĭ kəl). The letter that looks like an upside-down *e* (called a *schwa*) is pronounced like the *a* in *about*. You will find a key to the diacritical marks used in this book on the inside front cover.

3. **Derivation.** Information in brackets after the guide to pronunciation for a word gives further information about the source of that word. For example, after **diacritical** (dī ə krĭt´ ĭ kəl), under *dia* <G. "apart," would appear [*krinein* <G. "to separate"]. Thus, the word *diacritical* is made up of two words that come from Greek and means "separating the parts" and, consequently, "distinguishing."

4. **Familiar Words and Challenge Words.** Listed next to groups of defined words may be one or two sets of words belonging to the same family. You probably already know the Familiar Words in the shaded boxes. Try to figure out the meanings of the Challenge Words, and if you are curious, look them up in a dictionary.

5. **Nota Bene.** *Nota bene* means "note well" and is usually abbreviated to *N.B.* In *Vocabulary from Classical Roots*, NOTA BENE calls your attention informally to other words related to the theme of the lesson.

6. **Exercises.** The exercises help you determine how well you have learned the words in each lesson while also serving as practice for examinations such as the Scholastic Aptitude Test: synonyms and antonyms, analogies, and sentence completions. Further exercises illustrate words used in sentences, test recognition of roots, and offer writing practice.

---

*Reprinted from the student's edition of *Vocabulary from Classical Roots*

Introduction

The decline in American students' vocabularies and the decrease in Latin courses have caused vocabulary development books to flourish. Why one more? The authors of the *Vocabulary from Classical Roots* series found no book that fully served their purposes. Their students needed a book with a clear pattern of Greek and Latin roots to make more apparent the sources and the spelling of English words, a book with an organization to help students remember meanings as well as relationships, a book with challenging lessons.

The authors decided to transform their supplementary piecemeal handouts and lists of classical roots into a series of lessons with thematic coherence. In this volume, as in each book in the series, Greek and Latin words are grouped around a topic indicated by general headings: Taking the Measure (Numbers, All or Nothing, More or Less, and Before and After) and Enjoying (Creativity, Travel, Sports, and Animals).

Why the emphasis upon roots, since this is a book to improve vocabulary? The authors believe that Greek and Latin words have interest as forms in themselves. These words also reflect the way our language developed. When early humans had exhausted the supply of grunts and chirps for objects and actions, a more specialized classification of sounds began to signify *people, animal, fire, sky, earth*. Gradually a word like *earth* meant more than the ground people stood on; it meant the dirt they farmed or the land they saw stretching to the horizon. Much later, the word for *earth* in many languages meant the spinning ball that is humankind's home.

A study of roots—*classical* roots because their effect upon English has been so profound—reveals the complexity of transference from one language to another. What has disappeared in English is the picture or the action that the classical root conveys. The word *deviate* (Lesson 12) illustrates this point. *Deviate* comes from two Latin words: the preposition *de* meaning "away from" and the noun *via* meaning "road," "path," and so "journey." The literal definition of *deviate* is "to go away from the path." In English a person can deviate not only from a road or path, but also from rules, plans, an itinerary, etiquette, expectations, or habits. Many of the definitions in this book include both literal and metaphorical uses of words, sometimes to a student's surprise. The multiplicity of meaning can stimulate the imagination.

Vocabulary from Classical Roots introduces features not found in other vocabulary books:

• *Complete forms of Greek and Latin words.* Where other books give only root kernels (e.g., the Latin "fac" or "fect" meaning "make"), *Vocabulary from Classical Roots* provides complete forms—such as the principal parts of the verb *facio, facere, feci, factum,* meaning "to make" (Lesson 10). Knowing the various forms of this verb helps students understand why English derivatives like *faculty, factual,* and *perfect* belong to the same family.

• *Literary, historical, and geographical references.* Appearing in many of the illustrative sentences and exercises, these references help students become more culturally literate as they develop their vocabularies. A glossary identifying many of these references is located at the end of this teacher's guide.

• *Challenges to the curious. Vocabulary from Classical Roots* offers not only an overview of familiar words derived from specific roots but also more difficult words to challenge students, stimulating interest and independent exploration beyond the lesson itself.

• *Writing/discussion activities.* Every pair of lessons includes suggestions for creative or expository writing using words that students have learned. (See Combining Word Study and Writing, page 5.) The writing activities can also be used to stimulate discussion in the classroom.

Acquisition of new vocabulary words occurs in several stages: recognition and understanding of new words through reading followed by use of new words in speech and writing. This culminating stage requires much practice, which will be worth the time and effort, helping students develop fluency and confidence in their use of new words.

Teaching Suggestions

Teachers using *Vocabulary from Classical Roots—A* will naturally tailor the material to fit their courses. Carefully explaining the features of the book at the start can establish a pattern for students to follow; they will know what the book contains and what the teacher expects them to learn. Elements like diacritical marks will gradually become second nature in learning a lesson.

The teachers and students who have pilot-tested books in this series have been able to complete one book in a semester. Those who use Book A in a composition course that includes literature may extend work in the book over a longer period. Some teachers may choose to let students use the book individually at their own pace.

Whatever the pace, everyone profits by keeping the element of discovery alive. The temptation is great to fall into a pattern of checking exercises and asking questions about the words in a lesson. A process that becomes too predictable, however, lulls students into mechanical or insufficient preparation. At least one element of difference or surprise —supplementary information, a game, a contest—can help to maintain students' engagement with words.

GETTING STARTED (DAY 1)

1. Begin by pointing out that each pair of lessons has a *theme*, usually indicated by the title, to which all the roots in the lesson relate. Read the Latin motto and its English translation to the class and point out its relevance to the theme.

2. Help students see the *relationship* between the root and the familiar words and challenge words, as well as the key words.

   • You might begin a lesson by putting a root with many familiar words on the board (e.g., *unus*) and asking the class to name words they know that seem to relate to that root. Then have them look at the key words, familiar words, and challenge words given in the book. Students often express surprise that they already know so many of the words derived from a particular root.
   • Many students will become intrigued with the challenge words. Resist the temptation to define the words for those students. Refer them to a dictionary.

3. Ask students to *pronounce* the key words in the lesson by using the diacritical marks provided. Until students become familiar with these symbols, they will need help interpreting them. An explanation of the

diacritical marks is found on the inside front cover of this book and on the inside front cover of the student's book.

- Reinforce this initial pronunciation exercise throughout the week by finding ways to have students speak the words aloud every time you work on the lesson. The more times they speak a word or hear it used, the more likely they are to remember it and to have it become part of their active vocabularies.

4. Reassure students that the only words they are expected to *learn* are those defined in each lesson, the key words, and their varied forms.

5. Also assure students that they are expected only to *recognize* roots and know what they mean, *not* to memorize all the parts (for example, *facio, facere, feci, factum* in Lesson 10). *Vocabulary from Classical Roots* includes these different forms to show students that English words such as *affection* and *faculty* may look somewhat different but can have the same source. If your students have the time and interest to go more deeply into word formation, here are some suggestions for discussion:

- With a word such as *ars, artis* (Lesson 9), students may like to know that *ars*, or "art" is the subject in a Latin sentence; the change in spelling to *artis* accommodates a variety of endings indicating the grammatical role of the word in the sentence. (*Artis* means "of art.")
- The text gives the principal parts of all verbs: most verbs have four parts; a few, three. One of the most regular forms in Book A is *canto, cantare, cantavi, cantatum*, whose forms mean "I sing," "to sing," "I have sung," and "sung," the past participle (Lesson 9). One of the more irregular verbs is *pingo, pingere, pinxi, pinctum* meaning "to paint" in Lesson 10.

6. Read the *definitions* of the key words with the class, pointing out the following:

- Where varied forms follow the key word (e.g., under *monolith* in Lesson 1 comes the adjective *monolithic*), encourage students to pronounce all of the forms and practice using the variations in sentences.
- Where a key word has a strong positive or negative connotation, ask students to create situations and sentences illustrating the emotional quality of the word: *pretentious* and *preposterous* (Lesson 7); *artless* (Lesson 9); *resilient* and *valorous* (Lesson 14); *asinine* (Lesson 15).
- Where a key word has more than one meaning, particularly when it can be used both literally or metaphorically, help the students enjoy the difference. The word *omnivorous* in Lesson 3 offers a chance for playfulness: "eating both plants and meat" and "devouring everything." Students can consider their degree of omnivorousness—in matters of food, movies, music, books, or love of animals.

- Where a key word is a transitive verb (the word *transitive* appears as a key word in Lesson 11), you may wish to incorporate grammatical relationships. *Annihilate* in Lesson 4 serves well in such an exercise: what kinds of direct objects, noun or pronoun, might students like to annihilate, exercising their imaginations in colorful sentences?
- Help students be aware of *antonyms* that appear at the end of a number of entries. In Lesson 6, for example, *microcosm* is given below *macrocosm*. In Lesson 4 you might ask students to write in the word *covert*, "covered" or "hidden," at the foot of the entry on page 23.
- Where a related antonym appears under a key word (in Lesson 6 see *microcosm* listed under the defined word *macrocosm*), ask students to provide examples of both words.

USING THE EXERCISES (DAY 2)

1. Whether you assign the exercises as homework or class work, assign all the exercises in a lesson at one time in order to provide practice with every key word.

2. When correcting the exercises, students should hear synonym, antonym, and fill-in-the-blank questions and their right answers read aloud, rather than just the letter of the answer. This oral presentation reinforces correct pronunciation and use of a word in context. Important exceptions, however, are the B exercises, where one sentence in four uses the word incorrectly. Avoid having the incorrect sentence read aloud; instead give students the letter of the incorrect sentence and allow them to supply the correct word or a better word in these sentences, especially where words are similar in sound or spelling, as are *apiary* and *aviary* (Lesson 15).

3. Allow students time to ask questions about their errors.

FURTHER DEVELOPING THE LESSON (DAYS 3 AND 4)

1. **Combining word study and writing.** Practice in recognizing and using words in context and becoming familiar with Greek and Latin roots makes students better readers. Using new words makes students better writers. *Vocabulary from Classical Roots* encourages flexibility in writing through composing sentences and paragraphs in various ways. The examples given below, using the word *monolith* from Lesson 1, illustrate approaches to writing suggested in the text.

   A. Sentences using a key word:

   - Sentences that define, using a definition given in the text or, preferably, a paraphrase of the given definition

   Example: A **monolith** may be a huge slab of rock or a large business organization that has many offices or sections under one management.

• Sentences that supply a specific context

Examples: (1) Standing upright in a perfect circle, the **monoliths** represented an ancient system of measuring time based on the location of the sun.
(2) Although only seven stories high, the office building was the town **monolith**, casting a long shadow over the low buildings around it.

B. Sentences that imply the meaning of a key word:

Example: El Capitan, a huge block of granite rising 3,600 feet above the valley floor, regularly draws enterprising rock climbers to Yosemite National Park.

C. Paragraphs using a key word:

Example: Having invented a sweet bubbly drink that their neighbors raved about on hot days, the family began to advertise their product. Gradually it became so popular that billboards showed baseball players and movie stars drinking it. The inventors realized that with distribution throughout the world they had created a **monolith**.

D. Paragraphs that imply a key word:

Example: While traveling through the southwestern United States, we began to see enormous outcroppings of red rock standing like sentinels in the desert. We could see them from miles away and yet were amazed at their size as we drew closer. The wind whipped up clouds of dust and blew balls of tumbleweed at our tires and across the road in front of us, but the huge rock formations stood still and eternal in that endless space.

E. Paragraphs that explain derivation:

(These are especially productive when students are puzzled by the connection between the meaning of the key word and its root. Teachers and students may find this exercise more useful and lively if writers feel they can take a guess at the connection between root and word.)

Example: Since *monos* is the Greek word for "one" and *lithos* is the Greek word for "stone," *monolith* means "one stone." So why does *one* stone become a *large* stone in English? It may be because one stone appears large enough to be noticed, or important, like a mountain or something made of stone, such as a tall building.

Teachers can train students to avoid uninformative sentences like this one—That building is a **monolith**—an example of a *telling* sentence, one that provides no information to justify the word. Better by far is a sentence that provides a specific setting or situation and defines through concrete detail: a *showing* sentence.* Since many of the words that students learn in a vocabulary book are abstract and often ambiguous, sometimes having more than one meaning, students can benefit from associating visual or other sensory images with the words. Being specific lets students live closer to the pictures and actions implicit in the classical roots and encourages awareness of metaphor.

2. **Word games.** Playing word games with a lesson's key words and roots is enjoyable and also helps reinforce the meaning. Here are some suggestions:

   A. "Pictorial Charades." Modifying the rules of charades, students draw pictures that suggest a word from the lesson.

   B. "Scavenger Hunt." Ask members of competing teams where they would go to find a person or object from the lesson (e.g., Where would you go to see a pictograph? Hear a rhapsody? Find an artifact? Read an ode? Meet an artisan?) The answer should include a description of the person or object found.

   C. "Word Coins." A way to call attention to Latin and Greek sources of English words is invention of words from classical roots appearing in a pair or group of lessons. Students may use forms emphasized as roots of words in the lessons or less visible forms contained in brackets. The game consists of challenges to provide the best definition of the coined word (e.g., What might be the meaning of *polithy* [stone-selling]; *monopart* [having only one part]; *gramarchist* [handwriting expert]?).

3. **A vocabulary bulletin board display.** Make a display area where students can post newspaper and magazine clippings containing key words. This project usually grows rapidly and stimulates awareness of words in different contexts.

REVIEWING THE LESSON (DAY 5)

1. Most students benefit from reviewing for some form of quiz, which also permits both teachers and students to evaluate how well material has been absorbed. Here are some suggestions for quiz writing:

   • Review quizzes should include recognition of roots.
   • Do not limit a quiz to key words only; include other parts of speech derived from key words.

---

*Rebekah Caplan, *Writers in Training: A Guide to Developing a Composition Program* (Palo Alto, California: Dale Seymour Publications, 1984). The author makes clear distinctions between *telling* and *showing* and gives numerous suggestions for leading students away from "empty words" to clear, lively sentences.

- Ask questions that require paraphrase or sentence writing.
- Ask questions that require recognition of the different meanings of a single word.
- Divide students into groups of three or four to discuss meaning, derivation, and usage and to help one another to feel secure. The groups may take a second step by devising one or two questions that might appear on a test.

2. Some sample quiz questions for Lesson 1 follow.

SAMPLE QUIZ, LESSON 1

A. Analogies

   1. monogram : monolith ::
    a. duplicate : duplex
    b. unilateral : bilateral
    c. weight : organization
    (d.) letter : stone
    e. unanimous : monopoly

B. Fill-in-the-Blanks and Completions

   2. Both the roots __*monos*__ and __*unus*__ mean "one."

   3. As a result of this *bilateral* arrangement, our two schools now share the library resources, and librarians no longer have to purchase *duplicate* copies of expensive books.

C. Paraphrasing

   4. Paraphrase this sentence, substituting a word or phrase for the underlined parts so that the altered sentence means the same as the original.

     Because the <u>bipartisan</u> committee contained members with such conflicting ideas, they seldom came to <u>unanimous</u> decisions.

   5. Paraphrase this sentence, substituting words from Lesson 1 for the underlined parts so that the altered sentence means the same as the original.

     By <u>dividing</u> the ranch <u>into two equal parts</u> when they inherited it, neither sister gained a(n) <u>exclusive control</u> of the county cattle business. (*bisecting, monopoly*)

D. Sentence Writing

    6. Write two sentences that illustrate the different meanings of *monolith*.

    7. Write a sentence in which you use both *monologue* and *monopolize*.

FURTHER REVIEW

1. Because each two-lesson chapter has a common theme, an excellent time for a brief review quiz is the completion of each chapter (e.g., after even-numbered lessons). A sample quiz reviewing Lessons 1 and 2 is given below.

2. A cumulative review is recommended at the conclusion of Lesson 4 (covering 45 words), Lesson 8 (covering 83 words), Lesson 12 (covering 127 words), and Lesson 16 (covering the whole book, 170 words). Although the final number is substantial, regular review makes the words increasingly familiar.

SAMPLE REVIEW QUIZ, LESSONS 1 AND 2

A. Synonyms. Circle the letter of the word or phrase closest in meaning to that of the underlined word.

    1. quadrant   a. four-sided   (b.) one-fourth of a circle   c. four lines of poetry   d. a composition for four musicians   e. four-legged animal

    2. centenary   a. anniversary   b. guardian   c. group of 100   (d.) centennial   e. bicentennial

    3. triumvirate   a. made in three parts   b. three-sided   c. group of three musicians   (d.) group of three rulers   e. one-third

B. Antonyms. Circle the letter of the word or phrase most nearly opposite the underlined word.

    4. unanimous   a. dishonest   b. biased   (c.) in complete disagreement   d. dull   e. repetitious

    5. decimate   a. to mature   b. to lie   c. to encourage   (d.) to build up   e. to trust

    6. monopolize   (a.) share control   b. divide   c. decimate   d. converse   e. convert

C. **Multiple Choice.** Circle the letter of the word or phrase that most logically completes the sentence.

7. At his farewell performance, the actor delivered a long
_____ recalling the high points of his career.
   a. quatrain   b. monogram   (c.) monologue
   d. decathlon   e. trilogy

8. A _____ uniting the names of the couple decorated their
wedding cake.
   a. duplex   b. monolith   c. unilateral   (d.) monogram
   e. quadrant

9. This unusual _____ was composed of two sets of identical
twins.
   a. monopoly   b. quatrain   (c.) quartet   d. quadrant
   e. triumvirate

10. Competing in the ninth event of the _____, he injured his
leg and had to withdraw.
   a. bicentennial   (b.) decathlon   c. centenary
   d. monopoly   e. trilogy

11. One _____ of a circle contains 90 degrees.
   (a.) quadrant   b. quartet   c. trisection   d. bisection
   e. duplex

12. In 1976 the United States celebrated the _____ of the
American Revolution.
   a. centenary   b. triumvirate   c. monopoly
   d. centigrade   (e.) bicentennial

D. **Analogies.** Circle the letter of the pair of words or phrases that
have the same relationship.

13. bilateral : unilateral : :
   a. duplex : duplicate
   (b.) bicentennial : centenary
   c. bisect : trisect
   d. duplex : complex
   e. decimate : monopoly

14. duo : quatuor : :
   a. quadrant : duplicate
   b. monos : bi
   c. centigrade : fahrenheit
   d. decem : centum
   (e.) duet : quartet

15. athlete : decathlon : :
    a. trilogy : writer
    b. biologist : bisect
    (c.) musician : quartet
    d. monarch : rule
    e. altitude : quadrant

E. Sentence Completions. Fill in the blank with the most appropriate word from the list below. Use a word only once.

bilateral	decimate	monolithic	quartet
bipartisan	duplex	monologue	quatrain
bisect	duplicate	monopoly	trisect
decathlon	monarch	quadrant	unilateral

16. Archeologists rushed to _duplicate_ the Native American stone paintings before the waters of the new dam destroyed them.

17. The three hungry friends agreed to _trisect_ the pizza equally among themselves.

18. In order to have enough space for their large family, they converted a _duplex_ into a single-family dwelling.

19. Some fast-food chains are so _monolithic_ that hamburgers in Tokyo are guaranteed to taste the same as hamburgers in Moscow.

20. With the help of a _quadrant_, early settlers established that Mt. Washington was the highest point in the thirteen colonies.

21. Without consulting either her family or friends, she made a _unilateral_ decision to join the team.

22. Although they weigh only a few ounces, _monarchs_ migrate thousands of miles every year.

23. Anticipating early in the century that oil would replace coal as the main fuel for ships, Britain gained a _monopoly_ over oil fields in Persia.

24. The _quartet_ was made up of a soprano, a contralto, a tenor, and a bass.

25. Although the Romans did not often _decimate_ their legions, the custom of killing one in ten was used to inspire courage and loyalty.

Answers to Exercises

LESSON 1

EXERCISE 1A

1. b
2. e
3. b
4. d
5. e
6. b
7. a
8. b
9. c

EXERCISE 1B

1. c
2. d
3. c
4. a
5. a
6. b

EXERCISE 1C

1. monarch
2. monologue
3. monogram
4. unanimous
5. unilateral
6. bilateral
7. bipartisan
8. duplex

LESSON 2

EXERCISE 2A

1. a
2. a
3. d
4. b
5. e
6. d
7. e

EXERCISE 2B

1. trilogy
2. triumvirate
3. quartet
4. quatrain
5. decathlon
6. centigrade
7. bicentennial

EXERCISE 2C

1. *Trilogy*
2. decathlon
3. quatrain
4. trisect(ed)
5. quadrant
6. triumvirate
7. bicentennial
8. quartet
9. decimate(d)

REVIEW EXERCISES FOR LESSONS 1 AND 2

1. *monos, unus*
2. c
3. b
4. c
5. *duo, bi*
6. a. three-sided
   b. cut in four pieces
   c. 1000-year anniversary
   d. in 100 identical copies
   e. three-fold or a house for three families

LESSON 3

EXERCISE 3A

1. a
2. a
3. b
4. e
5. a
6. c
7. c
8. e
9. b

EXERCISE 3B

1. b
2. a
3. c
4. c

EXERCISE 3C

1. panacea
2. recluse
3. holocaust
4. omnipotence
5. pandemonium
6. cloister(ed)
7. omnipresent

LESSON 4

EXERCISE 4A

1. c
2. e
3. e
4. d
5. c
6. c

EXERCISE 4B

1. d
2. d
3. d
4. b

EXERCISE 4C

1. annihilate(d)
2. vaunt
3. inception
4. overt
5. aperture
6. nihilist
7. incipient
8. renegade

REVIEW EXERCISES FOR LESSONS 3 AND 4

1. *omnis, pan*
2. d
3. c
4. c
5. *vanus, vacuus*
6. to deny

LESSON 5

EXERCISE 5A

1. b
2. b
3. b
4. d
5. e
6. c
7. b
8. c
9. c
10. e

EXERCISE 5B

1. c
2. d
3. c
4. a
5. a
6. c

EXERCISE 5C

1. microcosm
2. expletive(s)
3. attenuate
4. microbe(s)
5. minutiae
6. satiate(d)

LESSON 6

EXERCISE 6A

1. e
2. a
3. a
4. a
5. b
6. a
7. a

EXERCISE 6B

1. b
2. b
3. c
4. b

EXERCISE 6C

1. magnate
2. polygamous
3. polygon
4. copious
5. macrocosm
6. megalomania
7. magnanimous(ly)

REVIEW EXERCISES FOR LESSONS 5 AND 6

1. e
2. e
3. *tenuare*, make thin
4. plenty
5. *magnus, megas*

Writing Activities

3.a. magnates . . . expletives . . . tenuous
3.b. minutiae . . . copious
3.c. minuscule . . . microcosm

LESSON 7

EXERCISE 7A

1. d
2. a
3. a
4. d
5. e
6. e

EXERCISE 7B

1. c
2. a
3. a
4. c
5. d
6. d

EXERCISE 7C

1. predestine
2. premonition
3. antebellum
4. precept(s)
5. anterior
6. avant-garde
7. pretentious
8. antecedent(s)
9. preempt(ed)

LESSON 8

EXERCISE 8A

1. d
2. b
3. a
4. b
5. e
6. a

EXERCISE 8B

1. c
2. c
3. d
4. c
5. b

EXERCISE 8C

1. posterior
2. posterity
3. posthumous
4. primate(s)
5. prime
6. premier(s)

REVIEW EXERCISES FOR LESSONS 7 AND 8

1. *primus*, first
2. *pre, ante*
3. first book; first school; an action that must come first
4. d
5. b

LESSON 9

EXERCISE 9A

1. a
2. b
3. d
4. a
5. c
6. e
7. d
8. d
9. d
10. e

EXERCISE 9B

1. a
2. b
3. b
4. d
5. c

EXERCISE 9C

1. artisan(s)
2. depict(ed)
3. parody
4. artifact(s)
5. ode
6. artifice
7. pictograph(s)

LESSON 10

EXERCISE 10A

1. c
2. e
3. d
4. a
5. b

EXERCISE 10B

1. c
2. d
3. c
4. d
5. b
6. c
7. d
8. c
9. a
10. b

REVIEW EXERCISES FOR LESSONS 9 AND 10

EXERCISE 1

1. b
2. d
3. b
4. a
5. c

EXERCISE 2

1. a. (could) mollify (the children)
   b. an efficacious (remedy)
   c. incantations . . . (waved overhead a) fetish
   d. (so) artless . . . (their) pretext
   e. (If you) recant

LESSON 11

EXERCISE 11A

1. a
2. c
3. c
4. a
5. c
6. a
7. b
8. e

EXERCISE 11B

1. a
2. c
3. c
4. b

EXERCISE 11C

1. episode(s)
2. transitory or transient
3. exodus
4. transitive
5. obituary
6. ambience

LESSON 12

EXERCISE 12A

1. c
2. a
3. c
4. d
5. a
6. c
7. c
8. e

EXERCISE 12B

1. d
2. c
3. b
4. b
5. b

EXERCISE 12C

1. advent
2. circumvent
3. deviate
4. convene(d)
5. itinerary
6. impervious

REVIEW EXERCISES FOR LESSONS 11 AND 12

1. a
2. d
3. e
4. a
5. c
6. journey
7. to come, to go

LESSON 13

EXERCISE 13A

1. b
2. e
3. b
4. d
5. e
6. b
7. b
8. d

EXERCISE 13B

1. b
2. d
3. a
4. b
5. a
6. c

EXERCISE 13C

1. conglomeration
2. celerity
3. interjection, ejaculation
4. abject
5. accelerate
6. concur

LESSON 14

EXERCISE 14A

1. d
2. d
3. a
4. e
5. a
6. d

EXERCISE 14B

1. c
2. d
3. a
4. c
5. d

EXERCISE 14C

1. desultory
2. prevalent
3. resilient
4. salient
5. voluble

REVIEW EXERCISES FOR LESSONS 13 AND 14

1. b
2. c
3. e
4. d
5. b

LESSON 15

EXERCISE 15A

1. d
2. b
3. c
4. e
5. b
6. c

EXERCISE 15B

1. c
2. d
3. b
4. a

EXERCISE 15C

1. capricious
2. equestrian(s)
3. apiary
4. equine
5. canine(s)
6. caper(s) or caprice(s)

LESSON 16

EXERCISE 16A

1. a
2. d
3. b
4. e
5. d
6. a
7. c

EXERCISE 16B

1. b
2. c
3. d
4. d
5. b
6. c

EXERCISE 16C

1. feline
2. piscine
3. zoology

REVIEW EXERCISES FOR LESSONS 15 AND 16

1. g
2. c
3. h
4. a
5. i
6. b
7. e
8. j
9. f
10. d

Glossary of Literary and Historical References

LESSON 1

2. monarch	Queen Victoria ruled the British Empire from 1837–1901, a period of peace and prosperity.
3. monogram	Napoleon Bonaparte (1769–1821) ruled France as the self-styled "Emperor of the French" from 1804 to 1815.
Exercise 1B, 1a	In 1918, following the defeat of the German Empire in World War I, Kaiser Wilhelm II (1859–1941) was deposed and the Weimar Republic, a constitutional democracy, was established to rule Germany.
Exercise 1B, 1c	Born in 1929, Queen Elizabeth II has ruled as constitutional monarch of Great Britain since 1952.
Exercise 1B, 2a	In *The Belle of Amherst*, a dramatic performance based on the life and poetry of Emily Dickinson (1830–1886), a single actor portrays the poet, who spent her life in Amherst, Massachusetts.
Exercise 1B, 2d	Two critical scenes between the two lovers immortalized in Shakespeare's play *Romeo and Juliet* take place on the balcony outside Juliet's bedroom.
Exercise 1B, 3a	In *1984*, George Orwell (1903–1950) depicts a future world in which individual liberties are restricted by a totalitarian state, personified by the ever-watching Big Brother.
Exercise 1B, 3b	The origins and purpose of Stonehenge, the circle of monoliths that stand on the Salisbury Plain of southern England, have invited centuries of speculation.
Exercise 1B, 6b	The neighboring countries of Poland, Latvia, and Estonia, along with Lithuania, are often referred to as Baltic states.
Exercise 1C, 1	Queen Lydia Kamekeha Liliuokalani (1838–1917) ruled the Hawaiian Islands from 1891 to 1893.
Exercise 1C, 2	In the Greek epic *The Odyssey*, its hero Odysseus recounts his experiences during warfare and his lengthy travels in a "flashback" during a banquet at the court of King Alcinous of Phaeacia.

LESSON 2

1. trilogy	Oxford philologist John Ronald Reuel Tolkien (1892–1973) wrote fantasy adventure novels, including the trilogy *The Lord of the Rings*, that incorporate the heroic material drawn from his academic studies.
3. triumvirate	Immediately following the fall of Julius Caesar in 44 B.C., power was jointly held by Mark Antony, Augustus Caesar, and Lepidus; by 30 B.C. Augustus had defeated the other two and established himself as the first Roman emperor.
9. bicentennial	The home of French rulers until the seventeenth century, the Louvre is now the principal art museum of Paris; its new wing of glass and steel was the subject of much controversy when it opened in 1988 during the bicentennial celebrations of the French Revolution.
Exercise 2C, 1	Set in the mythical kingdom of Earthsea, *The Earthsea Trilogy* by Ursula K. LeGuin (b. 1929) recounts the adventures of a young boy who must learn to use his magical powers wisely.

LESSON 3

1. pandemonium   In *Julius Caesar*, one of Shakespeare's Roman plays, the increasingly arrogant Caesar ignores warnings that the ides of March (the fifteenth) will bring danger to him, and he is stabbed by a group of conspirators in the Senate.

3. omnipotent   Lacking either military power or centralized authority, the Celtic tribes inhabiting Britain in the first century B.C. were easily conquered by the invading Roman army led by Julius Caesar.

8. totalitarian   Winner of a power struggle following the Russian Revolution of 1917, Joseph Stalin (1879–1953) held absolute authority in the Soviet Union until his death.

9. cloister   Transmitted by lice and fleas from infected rats, epidemics of Bubonic Plague, known also as the Black Plague or Black Death, swept across Europe during the late Middle Ages.

Exercise 3B, 4b   The animal stories and illustrations of Beatrix Potter (1866–1943) such as *The Tale of Peter Rabbit* and *The Tale of Mrs. Tittlemouse* are classics of children's literature.

Exercise 3C, 1   Since its development in the 1940s by Scottish biologist Alexander Fleming (1881–1955), penicillin has been the major drug used for treatment of infectious disease.

Exercise 3C, 2   Despite the objections of the Barrett family that Elizabeth could never marry, English poets Elizabeth Barrett Browning (1806–1861) and Robert Browning (1812–1889) eloped to Italy and raised a family there.

Exercise 3C, 3   A teenaged survivor of the concentration camp at Auschwitz, Elie Wiesel (b. 1928) has written extensively about the Holocaust.

Exercise 3C, 4   Montezuma II (1480?–1520), the last Aztec emperor of Mexico, was defeated by the Spanish conquistadores led by Hernando Cortes.

LESSON 4

3. annihilate   In 1938 American actor Orson Welles (1915–1985) broadcast a radio adaptation of H.G. Wells's (1866–1946) novel *The War of the Worlds* that created panic among listeners who believed it was a report of an actual Martian invasion.

5. negate   With his famous 1492 voyage that first brought Europeans to what is now called America, Christopher Columbus (1451–1506) established that ships sailing westward would not fall off the edge of the world.

8. vanity   Spanish artist Francisco José de Goya y Lucientes (1746–1828) is famous for his uncompromising portraits of the Spanish nobility as well as for his political paintings.

Exercise 4B, 1a   The literary reputation of English poet John Donne (1573–1631) rests on his erotic early poetry as well as his later holy sonnets and sermons.

Exercise 4B, 2a   Although she chose never to marry, English Queen Elizabeth I (1533–1603) was greatly influenced by a succession of male favorites who cultivated the monarch's vanity.

Exercise 4B, 2b   In *Pilgrim's Progress*, the allegorical tale of salvation by Puritan John Bunyan (1628–1688), the hero Christian must overcome many obstacles and temptations, such as the bazaar of Vanity Fair, on his journey to Heaven.

Exercise 4B, 3b   Because Russian nihilists of the 1860s and 1870s denied established authority such as the church and the monarchy and advocated acts of violence against these institutions, they were actively suppressed by the Czars, especially Nicholas II (1868–1918).

Exercise 4B, 4a   Nicolaus Copernicus (1473–1543) was the first scientist to advance the heliocentric model of the solar system.

Exercise 4C, 7   Italian educator Maria Montessori (1870–1952) established a method of early childhood education that stresses the child's own initiative in learning.

LESSON 5

8. comply   In 1955 Rosa Parks (b. 1923) defied a Montgomery, Alabama, ordinance by refusing to yield her seat in the front of a city bus; her arrest led a local minister, Dr. Martin Luther King, Jr. (1929–1968), to organize a boycott of the bus system.

9. implement   Invented by American manufacturer Cyrus Hall McCormick (1809–1884) in 1834, the reaping machine enabled one worker to harvest many acres single-handedly.

Exercise 5B, 2b   An advocate of nonviolence, Indian leader Mahatma Gandhi (1869–1948) frequently resorted to personal fasts as a means of influencing political events.

Exercise 5B, 2c   Blitzkrieg, or "the Blitz," was a series of intensive air raids launched by Germany against London during World War II for the purpose of demoralizing the populace and weakening English resistance.

LESSON 6

1. copious   The more than 1500 letters of Marie de Rabutin Chantal, Marquise de Sévigné (1626–1696), were published posthumously in 1725.

4. magnate   Western Union magnate Ezra Cornell (1807–1874) founded Cornell University in 1865.

Exercise 6B, 1c During the Third Reich, Adolph Hitler (1889–1945) required all German soldiers to swear an oath of allegiance to him personally rather than to the nation.

Exercise 6B, 2c As he expressed in his Gettysburg Address, Abraham Lincoln (1809–1865) urged a policy of reunification and tolerance between combatants after the Civil War.

Exercise 6B, 4c Alfred Nobel (1833–1896), the inventor of dynamite, provided in his will for annual prizes in the fields of literature, physiology or medicine, chemistry, physics, and the promotion of world peace.

Exercise 6C, 1   In the early twentieth century, William Randolph Hearst (1863–1951) built a powerful chain of American newspapers and magazines.

LESSON 7

1. antebellum	Written by Margaret Mitchell (1900–1949), *Gone with the Wind* was a best-selling novel that was made into an Academy Award-winning film.
2. antecedent	The Germanic language Anglo-Saxon (also called Old English), spoken in England between the eighth and twelfth centuries, is the primary source of modern English.
	One justification offered for the 1945 dropping of atomic bombs on the civilian populations of Hiroshima and Nagasaki was to hasten the surrender of Japan and the end of World War II.
4. avant-garde	An artistic style originating in late nineteenth-century France, Impressionism sought to capture a visual impression of a particular moment using pure primary colors and bold brushwork.
5. vanguard	The vastly outnumbered English troops of King Henry V (1387–1422) defeated an army of mounted French knights at Agincourt in 1415.
	In intentional contrast to the nobility, partisans of the French Revolution eschewed wigs and wore their hair unpowdered.
Exercise 7B, 1b	Following the stockmarket crash of 1929, a period of radical decline in the national economy known as the Great Depression caused thousands to be unemployed and millions to live in poverty.
Exercise 7B, 2b	In 1588 the English ships of Queen Elizabeth I defeated the "invincible" Armada sent by Spain's King Phillip II to conquer the English navy.
Exercise 7B, 2c	Both the public and private buildings of American architect Frank Lloyd Wright (1869–1959) illustrate his dictum that form should follow function.
Exercise 7B, 3d	Gautama Siddhartha (563?–483 B.C.?), whose title of The Buddha means "the enlightened one," taught the principles that became Buddhism, which include nonviolence to all living things.
Exercise 7B, 5a	In Shakespeare's play *Julius Caesar*, the protagonist defies several warnings, including his wife's dream, and attends the senate where an assassination awaits him.
Exercise 7C, 4	Although Polonius in Shakespeare's *Hamlet* is characterized by his long-windedness, his advice to his son Laertes has become famous: "And this above all, to thine own self be true. . . ."
Exercise 7C, 7	In Charles Dickens's novel *Little Dorrit* (1857), the impoverished Dorrit family illustrates the horrors of debtors' prisons and the folly of class snobbery.

LESSON 8

1. premier   Russian-born Golda Meir (1898–1978) emigrated first to the United States and then to Israel, where she served as Prime Minister from 1969–1974.

2. primate   After English King Henry VIII (1491–1547) denied the authority of the Pope in England, he appointed the Archbishop of Canterbury head of the newly established protestant Church of England.

8. posthumous   The journal kept by Anne Frank (1929–1945), a German Jewish teenager, during her family's years of hiding from Nazi internment has become a classic of Holocaust literature.

Exercise 8B, 1a   Charles Darwin (1809–1882) set forth his theory of evolution by natural selection in *On the Origin of Species* (1859).

Exercise 8B, 1c   American baseball player George Herman Ruth (1895–1948), who was known as "the Bambino" or "Babe," held the American League batting record for many years.

Exercise 8B, 2a   As a carrier of hemophilia, a genetic disease conveyed through the maternal line, Queen Victoria passed the disease on to many members of the royal family.

Exercise 8B, 3b   English poet Gerard Manley Hopkins (1844–1889) stopped writing and burned his youthful poetry when he was ordained a Jesuit priest. He returned to writing in the last years of his life, but these works were published only after his death by his friend, the poet laureate Robert Bridges.

Exercise 8B, 5a   American poet Henry Wadsworth Longfellow (1807–1882) is best known for his narrative poems on historical subjects such as *Evangeline, Hiawatha,* and *The Courtship of Miles Standish.*

Exercise 8C, 3   American author Edgar Allan Poe (1809–1849) wrote both famous poetry such as "The Raven" and suspenseful short stories such as "The Tell-Tale Heart" and "The Cask of Amontillado" as well as literary criticism.

LESSON 9

2. artifice   The Greek storyteller Aesop (620–560 B.C.) is credited as the author of *Aesop's Fables*. His sources were, however, probably earlier literature.

3. artless   Daughter of Prospero in *The Tempest* by Shakespeare (1564–1616), Miranda has never before seen a man other than her father and quickly falls in love with young Ferdinand, who has been shipwrecked on her island.

4. artisan   English craftsperson George Hepplewhite (d. 1786) designed and constructed cabinets, chairs, firescreens, and tables—the tables were often inlaid with woods of various colors.

5. ode   For poets of the Romantic period, among them Percy Bysshe Shelley (1792–1822), the ode was a familiar form allowing expression of personal feelings about nature.

6. parody   American writer Ogden Nash (1902–1971) is noted for his humorous verse, often marked by uneven line length and playful rhyme.

8. incantation   In the story "Ali Baba and the Forty Thieves" the incantation, "Open, Sesame," causes a rock in front of a cave to open like a door. Through this door comes a band of robbers carrying bags of gold. By overhearing this password, Ali Baba manages to acquire a fortune but cannot enjoy it until he has rid himself of the forty thieves. The story, one of Scheherazade's *Arabian Nights'* entertainments, so diverts the king that he does not indulge in his chronic habit of killing each new wife the day after the marriage. These Arabian, Indian, and Persian stories appeared between the eighth and sixteenth centuries; they began to be collected in the thirteenth century.

9. recant   Faced with pressure to conform to church belief in a geocentric rather than heliocentric universe, Galileo (1564–1642) recanted what he knew to be true.

10. depict   A colorfully embroidered strip of linen eighty yards long and nineteen inches wide, the medieval Bayeux Tapestry depicts events preceding and during the Norman Conquest of England (1066) when William the Conqueror defeated Harold the Saxon.

Jade Snow Wong (b. 1922) has said that she wrote *Fifth Chinese Daughter* (1950) in an attempt to create understanding between Chinese and Americans at a time when little had been written about the collision of cultures in the lives of young Chinese immigrants.

11. pictograph   Lasting for 2,000 years in Mexico and Central America, the Mayan civilization produced pyramids, a reliable calendar, and astrological observations as well as art forms preserved on stone monuments.

Exercise 9B, 1b   The Greek goddess Artemis, the twin sister of Apollo, is the moon goddess pledged to chastity, huntress and guardian of wild beasts, patroness of youth, and lover of music and dancing.

Exercise 9B, 1d   In Shakespeare's play *Macbeth* the three witches reveal to the title character the dramatic rise to power in store for him. This news stimulates him to hasten his acquisition of that power by taking the lives of those who appear to stand in his way: King Duncan, friend Banquo, and others.

Exercise 9B, 2d   Although Joan of Arc (1412?–1431), French saint and heroine, had led the forces of the Dauphin Charles VII to victory, she was judged to have violated religious principles with her visions and was burned at the stake.

Exercise 9B, 3a   Frankie Addams is the creation of American novelist Carson McCullers (1917–1967) in *The Member of the Wedding*. An adaptation of this novel won a Critic's Award in 1950 as the best play of the year.

Exercise 9B, 4a   Using the pseudonym Carolyn Keene, Harriet Stratemeyer Adams (1883?–1982) created mysteries for Nancy Drew to solve in forty-seven novels from *Secret of the Old Clock* in 1930 to *Invisible Intruder* in 1969. Continuing to use pseudonyms, Adams wrote other series familiar to many young people: Dana Girls, Hardy Boys, Bobbsey Twins, and Tom Swift Jr.

Exercise 9B, 4b   As described in Homer's ninth-century B.C. epic poem *The Odyssey*, Penelope successfully keeps her suitors at bay during her husband Odysseus's twenty-year absence.

Exercise 9B, 4c   Disguised as a man, Deborah Sampson (1760–1827) became a soldier in the Revolutionary War. Her identity was discovered, but she enlisted again, trained at West Point, and fought in combat, remaining unrecognized until she was hospitalized. Needing money to support her family in later years, she lectured about her war experiences to eager audiences.

Exercise 9C, 1   The Toltec civilization, which preceded the Aztec, practiced sun worship and human sacrifice. Its achievements included the building of pyramids, the smelting of metals, and the development of a calendar cycle.

Exercise 9C, 2   American artist Mary Cassatt (1845–1926) is best known for her paintings of women and children in a style influenced by the Impressionists.

Exercise 9C, 3   Ernest L. Thayer (1863–1940) tells Casey's story in thirteen four-line stanzas. Despite Casey's optimism, easy manner, proud bearing, and genial response to cheers ("he lightly doffed his hat" standing at the plate), the Mudville nine are out of luck (stanza thirteen) because "great Casey has struck out."

Exercise 9C, 6   Only the wily Moriarity poses real problems for Sherlock Holmes, the detective invented by Sir Arthur Conan Doyle (1859–1930).

LESSON 10

4. beneficence   By executive order of President John F. Kennedy, the Peace Corps came into being on March 1, 1961. At the request of governments around the world, it sends American citizens to assist with projects such as water supply and construction of dams in programs of health, agriculture, education, and community development.

5. efficacious   Samuel Johnson (1709–1784), English poet, essayist, and critic, became known for pithy statements in both conversation and writing. He was also the composer of the *Dictionary of the English Language* (1755), the first work offering definitions and examples of English words in use.

8. fetish   From *The Wonderful Wizard of Oz,* American author L. Frank Baum (1856-1919) went on to write thirteen sequels. His literary output of more than sixty books includes plays, tales, and articles.

9. faction   English author William Golding (b. 1911) depicts the struggles for dominance between two groups of marooned boys who vie for power as they wrangle over ways to survive.

10. mollify   The fable about the unmollified peacock is credited to Aesop.

11. context   The reason for hope to listeners of the Fifth Symphony was that in the first two measures of the first movement the sequence of notes (three eighth notes followed by a dotted half note) represents in Morse Code the letter *v* (dot-dot-dot-dash), the symbol for *victory*. German musician Ludwig von Beethoven (1770–1827) composed nine symphonies as well as concertos, sonatas, and other works.

Exercise 10B, 2a   John Philip Sousa (1854–1932), American composer and band master, became known as the "March King" for his military marches and band arrangements. One of his most familiar marches is "Stars and Stripes Forever."

Exercise 10B, 3d   American Lydia Pinkham (1819–1883) is best known as the inventor of a remedy for many physical complaints; it was a concoction of medicinal roots, seeds, and 18 percent alcohol.

Exercise 10B, 5c   Using the pseudonym Lewis Carroll, Charles Lutwidge Dodgson (1832–1898), English clergyman, parodied the style of heroic poetry in *The Hunting of the Snark.* The story tells of the search for the snark, an imaginary animal named Boojam, who is both elusive and dangerous. Carroll also entertained the children of friends with *Alice's Adventures in Wonderland.*

Exercise 10B, 5d   American artist Georgia O'Keeffe (1887–1986) has achieved recognition by the public as well as art connoisseurs. Her paintings of flowers and of landscapes of the southwestern United States appear often in reproductions on posters and calendars.

Exercise 10B, 6d   When Maya Lin, a Yale University student of architecture, first won approval for her design of the Vietnam War Memorial to be constructed on the Mall in Washington, D.C., objections were numerous. Opponents disliked the wide V shape, the black granite of the wall, and the absence of traditional military figures and inscriptions. However, since the dedication of the Memorial on November 19, 1982, public response has been overwhelmingly favorable toward the simplicity of the design and the long wall containing more than 58,000 names of dead and missing American men and women who served in Vietnam.

Exercise 10B, 9c   Homer (9th century B.C.) tells the story of the Trojan War in the epic poem *The Iliad*. After ten years of on-and-off warfare, the Greeks finally have the upper hand when the Trojans accept as a gift a huge wooden horse. Within its belly are Odysseus (Ulysses) and other Greek heroes who at night attack and conquer the city of Troy.

Exercise 10B, 9d   Without officially declaring war, Germany invaded Poland, Denmark, Norway, Belgium, the Netherlands, Luxembourg, and France in 1939 and 1940.

LESSON 11

1. transgress   In the first book of the Bible, Genesis, the serpent tempts Eve to eat the fruit of the tree of knowledge by saying, "For God doth know that in the day ye eat thereof, then your eyes shall be opened, and ye shall be as gods, knowing good and evil." When Adam joins Eve in violating God's command, both learn that they are banished forever from the Garden of Eden.

5. ambience   Although pollution has eroded the surfaces of statues and buildings, and the city itself is sinking—high tides seasonally flood St. Mark's Square— the city of Venice remains a lure to tourists and a historical and artistic landmark in Italy.

6. obituary   As a mother of nine children, Harriet Beecher Stowe (1811–1896) acquired experience which made her particularly sensitive to difficulties facing African-American slave women: unceasing work and the sorrows of separation from their children. *Uncle Tom's Cabin; or, Life among the Lowly* (1852) expresses Stowe's sympathy for the abolitionist cause.

9. erratic   In writing *Alice's Adventures in Wonderland* (1865) and *Through the Looking-Glass* (1872), Charles Lutwidge Dodgson (1832–1898), using the pseudonym Lewis Carroll, expresses something of the strangeness that many children feel in the process of growing up.

10. episode   Both a serious and a popular writer, Helen Hodgson Burnett (1849–1924) published *The Secret Garden* in 1911. Central character Mary Lennox discovers a secret garden, makes friends with a boy named Dickon, and helps another boy, the Rajah, recover from his illness through the beneficent effects of the garden.

11. exodus   During the years of the Spanish Civil War (1936–1939) fighting among diverse factions forced many people to leave the country. The war began when the Second Spanish Republic was overthrown by conservative forces. In 1939 General Francisco Franco led his Nationalists to power in Spain.

According to the Book of Exodus, God designates Moses to lead his people out of slavery in Egypt to the promised land Canaan. Although reluctant, Moses is successful, with God's help, in counteracting the difficulties his people and the Egyptian Pharaoh place in his way.

Exercise 11B, 1c   The company founded in New York by Louis Comfort Tiffany (1848–1933) developed methods and styles of glassmaking, producing stained glass windows and mosaics and introducing iridescent glass lamp shades and vases. An artist and patron of the arts, Tiffany also designed furniture and room decoration integrating patterns worked in stained glass.

Exercise 11B, 3a	Through rabbits' eyes, readers of *Watership Down* (1972) by Richard Adams (b. 1920) see human beings as unsympathetic aliens and a colony of rabbits as creatures possessing qualities familiar in human behavior—courage and cowardice, strength and weakness.
Exercise 11B, 3b	The presence of a group of African-American writers and artists in the New York City district of Harlem between 1919 and 1939 gave rise to what is now called the Harlem Renaissance.
Exercise 11C, 1	Mary Todd Lincoln (1818–1882) had a very difficult life. She was troubled by psychological problems early in her marriage to Abraham Lincoln, and she suffered intensely following the death of their son Willie in 1862, the assassination of President Lincoln in 1865, and the death of her youngest son Tad in 1871.
Exercise 11C, 5	Although during World War II Japan's Emperor Hirohito seemed an inimical figure to Americans, he was an influential proponent of unconditional surrender following the American bombing of two Japanese cities in 1945. Pressed by the Allies, he disavowed emperial divinity and became, according to the 1946 constitution, "a symbol of the state and of the unity of the people."
Exercise 11C, 6	Louisiana west of the Mississippi River belonged to Spain from 1769 to 1800.

LESSON 12

1. itinerant American pioneer John Chapman (1774–1845) became known as Johnny Appleseed because for forty years he traveled about in Ohio, Indiana, and Illinois distributing seeds and saplings.

2. itinerary Sacagawea (1784?–1884?), a member of the Oshone tribe, became a part of the Lewis and Clark exploring expedition from 1804 to 1806. Serving as a guide and translator, she also helped the company avoid catastrophe when they met some of her people on the journey.

One of the two highest peaks in the world, Annapurna, in the Himalaya mountain range, demands utmost care in preparation for a climb.

4. circumvent The heroine of Shakespeare's play *Twelfth Night*, Viola conceals her identity for protection, having reached a strange shore after a shipwreck. Dressed as a boy, she finds employment in the house of a duke, becomes the object of admiration of a gentlewoman Olivia, and discovers the twin brother she has given up for lost. All is well by the end of the play: Viola is herself and is loved by Duke Orsino.

6. intervene Mary Poppins' creator, Australian-born Pamela L. Travers (b. 1906), equips this character with magical powers and an umbrella whose handle is shaped like the head of a parrot.

The map of an island where treasure may be buried interests several characters in *Treasure Island* by Robert Louis Stevenson (1850–1894). Jim thwarts the miscreants who want the treasure as much as he, and through his daring he makes possible its return to the rightful owner.

9. devious *Walkabout* (1961) by Australian writer James Vance Marshall (1887–1964) contrasts the survival resources of an aboriginal youth undergoing his ritual walkabout and a stranded town-bred girl and boy whom he aids at a cost to himself.

Although the detectives Miss Marple and Hercule Poirot, created by Dame Agatha Christie (1891–1976), are different in temperament and way of life, they are equally quick in recognizing clues where mystery is concerned. Miss Marple is an elderly woman who lives in a small English village, and M. Poirot is a dapper, middle-aged Belgian and professional sleuth.

10. impervious Considered the founder of modern nursing, Florence Nightingale (1820–1910) resisted her family's pressures to stay in her native England and instead set out for the Crimea to serve British troops as a nurse. Facing inadequate supplies and horrendous conditions, she vowed to make changes in nursing procedures and became famous for improvements in nursing care.

Exercise 12B, 2b   Throughout *The Odyssey* by the Greek poet Homer (9th century B.C.), the goddess Athena serves Odysseus, giving him encouragement, creating disguises for him, and assisting his wife and son. With her help he returns to Ithaca after a twenty-year absence.

Exercise 12B, 2c   Dorothea Lange (1895–1965), American photographer, achieved prominence for her photographs of midwestern itinerants driven by duststorms to California in search of work. Ansel Adams (1902–1984), also American, experimented with light in his photographs, some of which include one of his favorite subjects, rock formations in Yosemite National Park in California.

Exercise 12B, 3d   Writing for both young people and adults, Madeleine L'Engle (b. 1918) has charmed her younger readers with *A Wrinkle in Time* (1962), *Journey with Jonah* (1967), and *A Ring of Endless Light* (1980), the last about young characters encountering the fifth dimension on their journey into space.

Exercise 12B, 5c   The first woman to cross the Atlantic in an airplane, Amelia Earhart (1897–1937?) earned subsequent world renown as the first woman to fly the same route solo.

Exercise 12B, 5d   Deciding that her life in England was too confining, Englishwoman Mary Kingsley (1862–1900) set out for West Africa where she often traveled by walking and swimming, meeting discomfort, disappointment, and terror along the way.

Exercise 12C, 5   Alejandro Malaspina (1754–1810?), Spanish explorer, led a scientific voyage to the Americas from 1789 to 1790. While conducting studies in Chile and Peru with his crew of scientists, he received new orders from Spain to look for a northern route between the Atlantic and Pacific Oceans. Although he failed to find such a route, on the return trip from Alaska he explored and made the first maps of the northern coast of America.

LESSON 13

2. celerity   In Greek mythology, Atalanta, huntress and voyager with the Argonauts, challenges each of her suitors to a footrace; losers are put to death, and the winner, Hippomones, becomes her husband. He, however, has tricked her by dropping along the way golden apples that she cannot resist picking up.

3. concur   In *Julius Caesar*, *Macbeth*, and *Hamlet*, the murder of a head of state or an event related to it occurs simultaneously with an aberration in nature.

4. discourse   With a treatise published in 1543, Polish astronomer Nicolaus Copernicus (1473–1543) explained his belief that the sun is the center of our solar system, with planets, including Earth, revolving around it. He contradicted the belief strongly held at the time that Earth is the center of the universe.

Although denied the formal education accessible to men, Margaret Fuller (1810–1850) read widely, became a journalist, wrote novels, and was a challenging conversationalist on subjects usually reserved for men. She achieved renown for her analysis of the role of women in *Woman in the Nineteenth Century*, published in 1845.

5. incur   As described by ninth-century B.C. poet Homer in *The Odyssey*, Odysseus and his men seek refuge in the cave of the one-eyed giant Polyphemus while on their way back to Ithaca after the Trojan War. By sending him into a stupor with strong wine, Odysseus is able to blind Polyphemus and devise a method of escape: clinging to the underside of rams that the giant sends out to graze.

7. succor   As a nurse, Clara Barton (1821–1912) assisted presidents and organized supplies and services for soldiers in the United States, Europe, and Cuba.

American novelist Louisa May Alcott (1832–1888) drew upon her own experiences in her portrait of Jo March, the eldest of four sisters in *Little Women*.

10. conjecture   Mentioned by Plato (427?–347 B.C.) as an island having a highly developed civilization but destroyed by an earthquake, the legendary Atlantis continues to tantalize scholars and stimulate research to determine if it existed.

Exercise 13B, 2b   In Luke 10:30–37, Christ uses the parable of the Good Samaritan to illustrate loving one's neighbor as oneself. The Samaritan in the parable is the third traveler to pass an injured robbery victim on the roadside but the first to give him aid by tending to his wounds, carrying him to an inn, and caring for him there. Although the Samaritan is traveling in unfriendly territory, he takes the risk of befriending the injured man.

Exercise 13B, 2c   Scotswoman Donaldina Cameron (1869–1968) saved or rescued many girls from slavery or concubinage in the vicinity of San Francisco even as late as the 1930s.

Exercise 13B, 4a   Although the creatures that "roared their terrible roars" in *Where the Wild Things Are* seemed to some parents and reviewers to be frightening to children, the book received the esteemed Caldecott Award in 1984. American author and illustrator Maurice Sendak (b. 1928) says that he tries to draw what children feel: pleasure, suffering, and defenselessness.

Exercise 13B, 6b   The Moors from Morocco introduced Arabic tradition in religion, art, language, and learning to Spain. Although flourishing there for seven centuries, Moors were expelled in the fifteenth century by King Ferdinand and Queen Isabella, who could no longer tolerate Muslim beliefs in solidly Catholic Spain.

LESSON 14

1. assail	The English word *quixotic*, meaning "visionary," "unrealistic," comes from the behavior and attitudes of Don Quixote, the character made famous by Spanish author Miguel de Cervantes (1547–1616). He is best known for *Don Quixote de la Mancha* (1605), whose title character believes himself designated to seek adventure in the style of outmoded chivalry. Riding his ancient horse, dressed in rusty armor, and accompanied by his servant Sancho Panza, Don Quixote is a ludicrous but endearing character.
3. exult	Born in 1927 in North Carolina and raised in Harlem, Althea Gibson caught the eye of tennis champion Alice Marble, who enabled her to break through the color barrier at tennis tournaments held at Forest Hills, New York.
4. resilient	A fall while racing destroyed the hopes of eighteen-year-old Jill Kinmont (b. 1937) to be a member of the 1956 Olympic ski team. Her story, told by E. G. Valens in *The Other Side of the Mountain* (1966), describes her ways of coping and compensating for her disappointment.
6. convalesce	Although recent medical studies cite a rise in cases of tuberculosis, a disease primarily of the lungs, it no longer means inevitable death, as was the case until the twentieth century.
7. avail	In more than 100 stories and novels, American author Horatio Alger (1832–1899) assures his readers that even the poorest boys, such as Ragged Dick and Tattered Tom, can rise to riches and respect if they work hard and do good deeds.
9. valor	Even when under German arrest with death imminent, Edith Cavell (1865–1915) did not refute the accusation that she had helped Allied soldiers escape imprisonment in Belgium. Her execution followed.
10. evolve	German printer Johann Gutenberg (1397?–1468) is considered to be the first European to use movable type in molds.
Exercise 14B, 1b	The battle between American and British forces at Fort Ticonderoga came early in the Revolutionary War, which lasted from 1775 to 1783.
Exercise 14B, 1d	British-born Jessica Mitford (b. 1917) criticizes the practices of funeral establishments in *The American Way of Death* (1963).
Exercise 14B, 3b	On its maiden voyage from England to New York, the British liner *Titanic* hit an iceberg and sank on April 14–15, 1912 with a loss of 1,517 lives. The fastest ship of the time, it was thought to be virtually invulnerable to accident.
Exercise 14B, 3d	The grandfather of Noah and the oldest person in the Bible, Methuselah is mentioned in Genesis 5:27.

Exercise 14B, 4a   The mechanical inventions of the Wright brothers, Wilbur (1867–1912) and Orville (1871–1948), evolved from bicycles to gliders to the first power-driven airplane, successfully flown at Kitty Hawk, North Carolina in December 1903.

Exercise 14B, 4b   Charles Darwin (1809–1882) and Alfred Wallace (1823–1913) appeared on the same platform in 1858 to explain the theory of evolution that their identical though independent studies had developed.

Exercise 14B, 4d   German-born physicist Albert Einstein (1879–1955) revised thinking about the physical universe, especially with the theory of relativity.

Exercise 14B, 5a   The properties of gold make it the most precious of metals and consequently a challenge to reproduce. Not only is it beautiful; it does not tarnish, and it is highly malleable, able to be beaten or thinned to a fraction of an inch without separating.

Exercise 14B, 5b   In his autobiography *Black Boy* (1944), Richard Wright (1908–1960) describes the impact of realizing the power of words in print. Passionate to read the work of Baltimore journalist H. L. Mencken, Wright prevailed upon a fellow employee to lend him a library card in 1920, a time when library privileges were denied to African-Americans in Memphis.

Exercise 14C, 4   In the story by Carlo Lorezzini (1826–1890) the artisan Gepetto carves a puppet named Pinocchio, whose nose grows longer whenever he tells a lie. French novelist Cyrano de Bergerac (1619–1655) became a legend for fighting whenever ridiculed for his long nose. He is the subject of the play *Cyrano de Bergerac* by French dramatist Edmond Rostand (1868–1918).

Exercise 14C, 5   The character of Fanny Flinching leaves the reader breathless with her nonstop talking in the novel by Charles Dickens (1812–1870).

LESSON 15

5. canine   Rin Tin Tin, an ex-German Army dog, first appeared in the film, *Where the North Begins* (1923), which was followed by other films and serials until 1930. The collie Lassie (actually a laddie named Pal) took title billing in *Lassie Come Home* (1942), based on a novel by Eric Knight. Production of Lassie films continued until 1962, along with television and cartoon series.

6. caper   Mr. Toad of Toad Hall, along with his companions Mole, Water Rat, and Badger, finds adventure along the River Thames in *The Wind in the Willows* by English author Kenneth Grahame (1859–1932).

7. caprice   In the comic strip *Peanuts*, American cartoonist Charles Schulz (b. 1922) has created characters who engage in perpetual one-upmanship. These include Lucy, Linus, Peppermint Patty, and the perennial victim Charlie Brown.

9. equine   French artist Rosa Bonheur (1822–1899) was the best known painter of animals in the nineteenth century.

11. equestrian   Robyn Smith (b. 1944) claimed the title of Best American Jockey from 1972 to 1978.

Exercise 15B, 1d   Emperor Charlemagne (742–814) held dominion over Frankish territory and as Emperor of the West (800–814) controlled a vast realm in what is now Europe. The painting of Mona Lisa by Leonardo da Vinci (1452–1519) is probably the most familiar piece of art on exhibition in the Louvre Museum in Paris.

Exercise 15B, 2b   Although Odysseus is disguised as a beggar, his old dog Argos recognizes his master after twenty years of absence during and after the Trojan War. Epic poet Homer lets the dog die moments later of old age and excitement.

Exercise 15B, 2c   Barbara Woodhouse (1910–1988) was so successful in explaining dog-training methods that her classes were filmed for television. Besides having the pleasure of watching dogs learn to behave, viewers appreciated Woodhouse's sensitivity to animals and her no-nonsense advice to ignorant or over-indulgent owners.

Exercise 15B, 3c   *Gone with the Wind* (1936) became a best-seller and the film (1939) starring Vivien Leigh, Clark Gable, and Leslie Howard was one of the most popular in movie history. American author Margaret Mitchell (1900–1949) had not taken her manuscript seriously; it reached an editor's desk only because of the enthusiasm of a friend.

Exercise 15C, 3   So-called "killer" bees are a strain released accidentally in South America where scientists in the 1950s were engaged in experiments. Advancing northward through Central America, Mexico, and into the United States, these insects are troublesome to human beings because of their severe stings and their displacement of native bees.

Exercise 15C, 4   Fictional horses Black Beauty and Black Stallion became the subjects of two well-known series, the first the work of Anna Sewell (1820–1878) and the second that of Walter Farley (b. 1915).

LESSON 16

1. feline	The Broadway musical *Cats* is based on poems written by T. S. Eliot (1888–1965), American-born poet, playwright, and literary critic.
3. lionize	Anthony Trollope (1815–1882) was one of several English writers who drew a large audience when they came to the United States to read from their work.
5. porcine	Miss Piggy is one of the many "Muppets" of American puppeteer Jim Henson (1936–1990), who was also the designer of Big Bird, Kermit the Frog, and Cookie Monster.
Exercise 16B, 1d	Writing under the pen name of George Orwell, Eric Blair (1903–1950) used fiction such as *Animal Farm* to highlight the dangers of revolution leading to totalitarian regimes such as that which occurred in Russia in 1917 and in Germany, Italy, and Spain in the 1930s. Orwell's novel *1984* envisions the consequences of the loss of individual freedom if Big Brother and Newspeak were to become a reality.
Exercise 16B, 2c	Thoroughly greased for her English Channel swim in 1926, Gertrude Ederly (b. 1906) set a record of fourteen hours and thirteen minutes even though bad weather forced her to swim thirty-five miles instead of the twenty-one miles separating France and England.
Exercise 16B, 2d	Although English writer Izaak Walton (1593–1683) was primarily a biographer, he is best known for his fishing expertise.
Exercise 16B, 3b	In an untitled poem about meeting a snake, American poet Emily Dickinson (1830–1886) says that for several of nature's creatures she feels a "transport of cordiality": "But never met this Fellow / Attended, or alone / Without a tighter breathing / And Zero at the bone."
Exercise 16B, 4b	The bear Winnie the Pooh, Piglet, and the donkey Eeyore figure in the children's book by English writer, A. A. Milne (1882–1956).
Exercise 16B, 5c	The Beatles, a British rock group that became a musical phenomenon in 1962, were John Lennon, George Harrison, Paul McCartney, and Ringo Starr. Members of the original Supremes were Diana Ross, Mary Birdsong, Florence Ballard, and Mary Wilson.
Exercise 16B, 6a	Jane Goodall (b. 1934) describes her studies of chimpanzees in several books, one of which is *My Friends, the Wild Chimpanzees* (1967). In *Gorillas in the Mist*, published in 1983, Dian Fossey (1932–1985) gives an account of her fifteen years in Africa studying gorilla habits and habitats.
Exercise 16B, 6d	With the publication of *On the Origin of Species* in 1859, Charles Darwin (1809–1882) prepared the way for controversy about the origins of hu-

man life. Several distinguished scientists supported Darwin's contention that humans and the lesser primates have evolved from a common ancestor, an idea that shocked believers in God's creation of Adam and Eve as described in the first chapter of Genesis.